MW01268446

The
When|Win
Approach

The Formula To Overcoming Life's Challenges

_____

LaShaundria Coleman

Foreword By Les Brown

The When|Win Approach

"The Formula To Overcoming Life's Challenges"

Contact@TheWhenWinApproach.com
www.TheWhenWinApproach.com
404-482-2930

Ordering Information: Quantity sales. Special discounts are available on quantity purchases by corporations, associations, and others. For details, contact the "Quality Sales Department" at Info@TheWhenWinApproach.com

ISBN (978-0-692-87834-7)

Dedication

You are the best thing that has ever happened to me. You've given my life purpose and inspired me to strive for greatness. You are my why, the reason I exist. You've witnessed me overcome many of life's obstacles. Fight for what you want in life; be unstoppable. I believe in you and your unlimited potential. Create your own success; you don't need any credentials. You can defy all the odds and overcome any situation. You have so much greatness within you; the world is waiting...Show up! I dedicate this book to you King Jimmie Jayvonn Royster My Forever Love !!

Table of Contents

Acknowledgments

I thank God for guiding my footsteps during both certain and uncertain times. I am humbly grateful for the love, grace, and mercy bestowed upon me. I thank my higher power for all that is and who I have become.

I express my earnest gratitude and love to Mr. Les Brown. His teaching has been instrumental in the reform of my life. Thank you for touching my heart, igniting my spirit, and always encouraging me to transform my mindset. Thank you for training me and equipping me with the tools I needed to go out and speak with confidence, purpose, and passion. You are truly one of the greatest speakers of our times, and I am genuinely blessed to be one of your students. Because of you, I aspire to inspire until I expire.

For my Son, Jimmie, my one and only son. Your life depends on my efforts and I changed as a result of that primary fact. I wanted you to see the over-comer in me and know that you too can overcome any obstacle that life throws in your way. I am not what my past made of me nor are you. I reconstructed my life to become a product of my decisions rather than the conditions and environment around me. I believe that you too can change your life and rise above and beyond any level of success that I have and can attain. You have unlimited potential, I believe in you. When/At and/or during which time you make necessary positive adjustments to your life, you will be successful in achieving your desired end result, Win. I Love You with all my heart.

Mom

To my beautiful Queen LaShanda. I feel blessed to have such a supportive and inspiration partner. Thank you for standing by my side and believing in me throughout this new journey. This is one of many new beginnings that we will share together. I look forward to supporting you in your business endeavors as well. I Love You Cree, Courtney, and Cameron, more than words can express.

To my parents Zettie "Smith" Perry, and Charles Perry. Mom, thank you for being the epitome of strength. Without your display of power and courage, I would not know how to powerfully maneuver through life. It brings me great joy to see that you are finally letting go of your fears so you can live the life of your dreams. The best is yet to come. Dad, thank you for always believing in me and supporting all of my business endeavors. Although you are not physically here with me, I know that you are watching over me. Thank you for your continued support.

To my siblings. Brother Byron, may you rest in paradise as your peaceful spirit lives on vicariously through me. Through your relentless determination, I learned the importance of being ambitious and never giving up, thank you, because of you, I know how to defy the odds and just go, in the direction of my goals and dreams. I miss you and Dad more than words can express, and I love the both of you dearly.

Orlando (Carol) Smith, thank you both for holding me down and making me smile even in the face of adversity. Saia HuKeekui, thank you for sharing your knowledge and wisdom with me. Also, thank you for helping me edit my book. Respect and infinite blessings Queen. Nicole (Johnal) Gleen, my fellow dreamer, we have been dreaming and setting goals together since childhood, let's continue to make

LaShaundria Coleman

our dreams our reality, Thank you for always believing in me. LaSheda Perry, Cynthia Perry, Charles Perry Jr., Rachelle Renford, Vonceal Renford, William Coleman, and Charlene Perry, our parents did not raise any quitters. I believe in you all. Don't settle. To my first cousin Algie Turner, you're like a brother to me. Thank you for always looking out for your lil sis when I needed it most.

To all my beautiful nieces and nephews, to many to name individually, please know that you are all very special to me and I want you to know that I believe in you all. Never allow anything to come between you and your dreams, anything is possible.

To all that I have mentioned, keep pressing forward until you Win...keep going! Never give up no matter how hard it gets.

9

It is still possible for each and every one of you to accomplish your goals and dreams.

I never thought I would lose so many people I cared about in such a short period of time. Tajuana "Abby" Smith, Nakeecha "Keecha" Hayes, Kheyarra Williams, Anthony "Tony" Sheard, Angela Crawford, Jamel Davis, John D. Smith Sr, Lee V. Smith, Mary O Smith, Clinton Smith, Mamie Paul Coleman, Cortez "Peeper" Hill, Jamaul James, Stephanie Pugh, Annie Hayes, Joshua Hayes, Yolanda Sankey and Shirley Allen. I enjoyed the time we shared together. Even though your existence was brief, it inspired me to turn over this new leaf. You did not die in vain. Through your deaths, I found life and so will many others. Rest in Paradise, until we meet again. Love Always.

To my readers, thank you for purchasing my book. My dream would not be a reality without God's grace and your support. I appreciate you allowing me to share my approach to overcoming life's challenges and experiences in an effort to help you learn from my mistakes and temporary defeat. If I can bounce back from a tough situation and Win so can you. I'm leaving the ball in your court. When you make a conscious decision to create positive change in your life, you will Win and be successful in achieving your desired results in life.

At or during which time you change, you will gain a victorious attitude and lifestyle. The When|Win Approach.

With Love,
Thank you all

Foreword
By Les Brown

It has been said that it doesn't matter what happens to you in life. What matters most is what are you going to do about it. LaShaundria - mother, speaker, and entrepreneur - is a shining example of what we can become in spite of our environment, circumstances, and bad choices. That none of those things define who we really are. From selling drugs and using them and doing time behind bars, she proves at any moment you have the power to turn your life around. This book proves that where there's a will, there's a way, no matter how low you have fallen. Armed with a sense of purpose and a deep, unstoppable desire to make something of her life, she shows us how we literally have the power to snatch victory from the jaws of defeat.

LaShaundria tells it like it is in her raw, transparent, and authentic approach. She takes us on a journey into the world of drugs and what it's like to live life on the wild side.

Each chapter brings us up close and personal to what life is like for those that are seen as lost souls with very little hope. LaShaundria has gone through the storms of life and has lived to tell it and has decided that she's going to live her life as an example of how we all can change at any given moment. You have something special within you – greatness.

This book will bring out your greatness. This book will give you the path, methods, and techniques to create a new chapter for yourself. My name is Les Brown, and this book changed my life and I'm sure it will change yours. I highly recommend it. LaShaundria I am proud of you.

Introduction

"We cannot become what we want to be by remaining what

we are" ~**Max DePree**

At or during which time you let go of the negative, you will gain the positive. At or during which time you release the old, you will achieve the new. At or during which time you release what you believe to be good, you will accomplish greatness. At or during which time you change, you will gain a winning attitude and lifestyle. In essence When|Win.

One of the greatest lessons I learned in life was When I realized that I can Win. You will Win "not if" however, When you realize that you have the power inside of you to do so.

Chapter One

When I Was Born

She's not breathing yelled the nurse. Rush her to oxygen. January 18, 1979, 10:15 a.m. at Niagara Falls Memorial Medical Center. I made my entry into this world by the grace of God. The medical staff helped me to breath. I was born into a single parent household of four. I was the second to youngest child.

At the age of three, my mother noticed that I dragged my right foot and had a limp when I walked. She took me to see doctor after doctor yet they were unable to determine a cause, diagnosis, or cure. I blamed it on the doctor constantly tapping my kneecaps with his plexor during my visits.

However, later on in life, I found out that my condition resulted from my brain not receiving enough oxygen when I was born. The lack of oxygen killed my nerves that correspond with my lower limbs. I have limited function in my right leg. I also walk with a very noticeable limp and my entire right foot is deformed. The doctor advised me that I would be wheelchair bound at a very early age as a result of my condition.

As a child, I was singled out at school because I was different from all the other girls. You know how the story goes. Naturally, I was the last one to get picked for a kickball game if I even got picked at all. I remember in elementary school my gym teachers would make me sit out of most of the gym activities. The boys and girls used to tease me and call me handicap, cripple, and mocked the way that I walked. I used to get into a lot of physical altercations with kids defending myself. I faced a lot of self-esteem and confidence issues as a result of enduring constant ridicule as a child. I wasn't only teased by my peers, but it also happened with adults in my family as well. My childhood was filled with a lot of unpleasant memories mostly related to how imperfect everyone said I was.

In 1986, my mother met my step-dad and we moved to Cleveland, Ohio. They got married several months later. My step-dad had three children that were living on the streets of Alabama by themselves. The very next day after my mom married my step-dad, they drove to Alabama and picked up his three children and brought them back to live with us in Cleveland. Our household size automatically increased to ten.

Like a majority of inner-city African American families, mine too was affected by the crack epidemic in the early 80s to mid-1990s. My parents struggled with addiction for a number of years. They did not have careers; they worked a number of dead-end jobs to make ends meet. There were plenty of occasions when we wondered where the next meal was coming from.

My dad used to get on his bicycle in the middle of winter and ride around to find work so he could provide us with meals. Poverty was a familiar theme in our household. My oldest brother moved out and went to live with my grandmother. Being that it was seven children to provide for with no study jobs, we experienced lack. Not only did we lack the main necessities for survival, but we suffered emotionally as well.

When I was growing up, I did not know anything about potential. I can't recall being taught the word in school nor did I hear the word used on my sibling and me at home. I didn't have anyone there to encourage me to be my best, do my best or just simply to inspire me to want to win. I was not familiar with the concept of being successful because I did not have any successful people in my immediate surrounding to identify with. Throughout my childhood, I measured success with material things. As a result of the environment that I grew up in, I viewed individuals such as the neighborhood drug dealers as successful.

Like millions of African-American youth that dwell in undesirable social conditions that glorify the drug lifestyle, I too became a product of my environment. Growing up on the wrong street in New York will surely change your life forever. I was exposed to drugs all my life; my parents used them and

I heard stories of my older brother selling them once he left home. I just had never seen, touched or sold them until I was introduced to the drug game at age eleven when we moved back to Niagara Falls, New York. I was not old enough to get searched or go to jail, so my older cousins would have me hold their drugs for them while they hustled on the block. I used to get what I thought were good benefits from this arrangement, so I was sold. I was searching for a way out of the lifestyle of poverty that I was so used to, but not content with. Plus that was just the way of life. My parents were too distracted with their own habits to pay attention to what I was doing.

Chapter Two

When I Was Younger

When I was twelve years old, my younger sister and I witnessed my mother experience a tragic accident. She was attempting to fill her lighter with fluid when some spilled on her nightgown. Not noticing the leak, she lit the lighter and it caught fire. After hearing her gut wrenching screams, my sister and I ran outside our bedroom door where we saw pieces of her purple nightgown still burning. We ran into her room and she was under a cover crying. I could see pink flesh showing from underneath the blanket. She told us that she was okay and to go back to our rooms.

We did so hesitantly, filled with fear and concern. We walked back past the burnt gown and went into our room. My sister and I sat there in tears and silence as we heard the commotion of my step-dad helping her downstairs to take her to the hospital. That night the stench of lighter fluid and burnt skin lingered in the air. I didn't realize that my mother injuries were as bad as they were until we went to visit her. She spent several months in the Critical Care Unit at ECMC hospital's burn unit. I'll never forget the smell of the burn unit and the intense wash downs and gown, gloves, mask, and shoe covers that we had to wear before entering to see her.

During the time that my mother was hospitalized, my life took a turn for the worst. Instead of holding drugs for my cousins, I began breaking off pieces of their cookies, selling them for myself and keeping the profits. I did that for a while until my cousins felt that the loss they were taking was

22

greater than making a sale to an undercover and getting caught with the drugs on them. That was not the introduction to the hustler in me because years prior to that I was always doing something to make money. I played lottery numbers for my elders, collected bottles, picked worms for the fishers. I did whatever it took to earn money. That was just my introduction to fast money.

I've always had an entrepreneurial spirit. However, when I was younger, I was not taught how to use my skills effectively. My mother was hospitalized, my dad was watching us, but we were pretty much watching ourselves. I was in seventh grade at the time. I did not value my education, so I dropped out of school at the age of thirteen, and began selling drugs full time. Because of my age, the state mandated me to attend school via tutor, alternative school, etc. Needless to say my unchanneled anger and bottled up emotions caused me to get expelled from every program I attended.

We lived on Linwood Avenue in Niagara Falls, New York. The entire neighborhood was infested with drugs, crime, and violence. At one point my family had over seven houses on the block and was selling drugs out of every single one of them.

We moved from midtown to the east side of the city when I was around fourteen years old. I thought we were moving into a better environment with little to no drug activity. Come to find out we moved into the heart of one of the hottest blocks on the east side. It was business as usual. We lived on 15th and East Falls Street in a three-story apartment building filled with drug activity. The street was a dead end full of apartment buildings, and almost every house on the block had some

24

form of drug activity. We lived in a 24hr, 7day a week, 365 days a year nonstop trap house.

During the course of living on 15th Street, I met two individuals that I formed great friendships with. Both lived on the block and were my best friends at one point or another. One was named Art, and the other was Mel. Art had moved to New York from Philly with his mother's boyfriend. His mother was incarcerated and she was experiencing kidney failure at the time; she eventually passed away. Mel had moved to Niagara Falls from the Bronx, New York. He was living with his aunt because his mother was battling drug addiction. I bonded with each of them like they were my little brothers. I was older than both of them so most of the time they followed my lead. They looked up to me and held me down to the fullest. I remember instances where they both made sacrifices to make sure I was good. And vice versa, I made sure they were good—when I ate, we all ate together.

No one could tell me any different. I just knew I was winning during my teenage years. My parents were distracted doing their own thing. Meanwhile, I was my own boss and had workers under me. I was getting money and a lot of it for a youngster. I was able to provide for my sister and brother as well as my close friends. We used to go shopping at the Rainbow mall and Main Place mall in Buffalo almost every day. We ate whatever we wanted, whenever we wanted. I felt that I had escaped the life of poverty that I resented so much. Because I had the money, fancy clothes, car, etc., the individuals that I surrounded myself with gave me a false sense of accomplishment. During this period of my life, winning was associated with what you had. I never thought of it in terms of a spiritual or emotional space or state of mind.

I lived a fast lifestyle for about four years before it caught up to me in 1996. I'll never forget it; I was at my oldest brother house. I woke up out of my sleep to use the bathroom and on the way, there were Niagara's Most Wanted Newspaper clipping of myself all the way down the hall leading to the bathroom. My brother had posted them up; he just watched me look on in shock and laughed. I eventually turned myself in and was sentenced to one year in Niagara County Jail. There I was at the age of 17, receiving my first strike, my first felony conviction. During the time I should have been graduating with my peers walking across the stage accepting my high school diploma, I was incarcerated, locked up in a cage. I never experienced class day, prom or any high school activities. High school was foreign to me.

I was incarcerated with several family members, including my mom. All six of us served time together. My older cousin

Juana used to look out for me like she did when we were free. She was one of my older cousins who had schooled me to the game. She was smart, sexy, sophisticated, and always one step ahead of the game. Anytime I was locked away in solitary confinement, she would sneak me food and candy because she had created relationships with the correctional officers and become a trustee. We all eventually served our time and were released.

Because I dropped out of school in the seventh grade, I obtained my GED while I was incarcerated. I was released when I was close to eighteen. When you are sentenced to one year, you actually serve ten months because you get two months reduced for good time. Upon my release, I made a vow to myself that I would not get involved in the drug lifestyle again. When I returned home, everyone was doing the same exact things they were doing when I left. It was like a year hadn't passed and it was just the next day after I left.

Instead of diving head first back into the game, I enrolled at Niagara County Community College and pursued a degree in Computer Science. I found out that I was with child a few months later. I was excited about being a new parent; however, I was concerned about how I was going to provide for my unborn child. Forced with a decision to work a minimum wage job and barely get by or go for what I know and live in my illusion of thriving, I chose the latter and dropped out of college.

I took my new role as a soon-to-be-mother very seriously. I was determined to give my unborn child the life I only dreamed of. I did not want him to experience the hurt, pain, and disappointment that I had experienced. I wanted him to go down a different path than I had. I hustled to get everything I needed for my newborn. I set up a full Looney Tunes nursery video camera, intercoms, and the works. My son Jimmie Jayvonn arrived on August 15, 1996. That truly was the best day of my life. I never imagined being a parent up until that point. Something inside of me changed. I did not want to live the lifestyle that I had been living anymore. I wanted to do better, be better so that I could allow my son to see better than I had.

After I had obtained everything I needed for my unborn child, I got back out of the game. Only to turn right back around and get back in it several months later. As a result of me being in an abusive relationship and having every single resource that I had taken away from me, I literally was down to my last few diapers for my son when I made the decision to start over.

I was on the phone with my cousin Kalisha. She lived in Atlanta at the time. I was stressing my situation, she was talking about hers, and we decided to work together to hustle up the money that we needed to survive. We would do that for a while then register for college. My mom began keeping my son for me temporarily. I put our belongings in storage. Kalisha moved back to Niagara Falls from Atlanta. We leased a two bedroom trap house together in midtown. We executed our plan. We were bringing in a lot of revenue. We hustled, and took a cut from allowing people to gamble at our spot too. We had dice games and multiple card tables set up. We had a 24hour a day, 7days a week trap house.

Kalisha had been exposed to the drug lifestyle because her mother was a notorious user. We grew up across the hall from one another. Our parents actually used to get together. I remember we used to be so hungry that we would walk across the train tracks to a house across the street from Center Court projects to steal vegetables out of the garden. It was the house behind the Center court store. We would come home, wash them, cut them up, and eat them. We had all been exposed to drugs; however, I hate to admit, but I was the one who showed her how to sell them.

We were balling out of control. We had one of the most lucrative trap houses in the city at the time. We did whatever we wanted. We spent thousands of dollars shopping whenever we wanted; we went to clubs every weekend and popped bottles. We were living a very fast lifestyle at a young age.

My maternal instinct wouldn't let me stay there. As we had planned, I wanted to get out, get my son and house back so I could enroll in school and work. We ended up letting the trap house go and going our separate ways. I enrolled in college, but Kalisha stayed in the game.

I was eager to re-create my life for the betterment of my son. My mother helped care for him while I studied Business Management at Bryant & Stratton College in Buffalo, New York. Attending Bryant & Stratton College was a turning point in my life.

There were professors and admissions representatives there that made an impressionable impact on my life. They challenged me to dig deep within myself to unearth the authentic me. They helped me to realize that there was a world outside of my neighborhood. They helped me to believe in myself and focus on using my untapped potential. My English professor helped me to cultivate my writing skills. They exposed me to ways of thinking and concepts that I hadn't been exposed to before.

Chapter Three

When

I Did Not Have Faith

College allowed me to meet new people whose lives were heading in the right direction. I was doing so well my first semester that I made dean's list. I knew I was changing my life for the better. Everything was going well. I had just found an apartment for my son and I. A few days before I was scheduled to move in, I received a phone call from Brandon, an old acquaintance that used to spend a lot of money with me. He had disappeared owing me a couple thousand dollars.

The first thing he explained was that he wanted to take care of his debt, he went on to ask me about making a purchase. I advised him that I didn't sell drugs anymore. He said, "Alright, you can come pick up your money." Instead of keeping my faith and commitment to myself and my higher power to no longer affiliate with the lifestyle to any capacity, I said, "Ok, I'm on my way." I was in the car with my son and a friend and her daughter at the time. I didn't feel comfortable riding to pick up my money with the kids in the car, so I asked this guy I knew to drive me.

We pulled up to Brandon's house, and an unknown white male was standing outside. I told the driver that I didn't know that guy. As he approached the vehicle, I advised the driver not to talk to him. He rolled down the window anyway. He came to the back window where I was at, pulled out a bankroll and said: "Brandon told me to give this to you." I

just looked at him strangely and wouldn't take it. At this point,

I felt like he was the police I didn't want to talk to him

because he could have had on a wire. I wouldn't take the

money from him. I told the driver to pull off. The money

hungry driver just saw the money in his hand and wanted it

from him. He told me to open the door for the guy. I said no

and slid to the opposite side of the car. I didn't know him; I

didn't trust him. There was a guy riding in the front seat, he

reached back and unlocked the door. The guy eagerly hopped

in the back and began to ask for drugs. I wouldn't talk, I was

so angry. The driver was not listening to me and was so

money hungry that he was jeopardizing all of our safety.

Brandon was nowhere to be seen and I didn't know this guy

sitting in the car with us now; I told the driver to pull off

multiple times.

The guy made a hand to hand purchase from the driver once he got in, then he proceeded to encourage the guy to buy more when he pulled out his service pistol and placed it on the back of the driver's skull and said: "Don't you ******* move or I'll blow your ******* brains out." I screamed, "Pull off. Driveeee." The driver was stuck like a deer in headlights, and in a blink of an eye, the entire car was surrounded by police cruisers and officers aiming their guns at our heads.

I was taken to Erie County Holding Center and given a $20,000 bail. I had been the intended target, but I didn't make the sale or receive the money. I admit I was in the process of moving, pressed for cash, and made an unwise decision to turn to my past and it came back to haunt me. Had I just kept the commitment I'd made to my higher power, I would not have been in that predicament. Had I just kept my faith I would have been alright because I received a $4,000 school refund check the very next day. Needless to say, I couldn't cash it because I was locked up. I eventually got bailed out. I stayed enrolled in college and worked on campus in the library during the time I was out on bail. My English Professor and admission advisor fought for me. They stood with me at my court dates, wrote character reference letters, and even offered alternative sentencing options. I received a 3 to 6-year sentence anyway.

New York State Department of Corrections transferred me to Bedford Hills maximum security prison. That was an experience that I will never forget. It was raining cats and dogs when the bus pulled up to the prison. The first thing I noticed was the graveyard with makeshift headstones across the street. The next thing that caught my attention was the gargantuan prison. I had been to jail before but never a maximum security facility of that size. My stay there was supposed to be brief. However, I got lost in the system and ended up spending several months there. I was ultimately transferred to Albion Correctional Facility then to Lakeview Shock Incarceration Correctional facility. Lakeview Shock is a minimum security boot camp program that reduces the sentence of non-violent offenders to 6 months upon completing the program. The program is extremely physically and mentally intense. I was medically disqualified as a result of my medical condition. I was devastated yet not defeated. I was determined to complete the six-month program as opposed to going back to prison and serving a three to six-year sentence. I wrote the Superintendent a letter pleading to participate in the program. I assured him that I was physically capable of successfully completing the program. The Superintendent gave me the opportunity and I ran with it. I must admit, Shock was one of the most physically and mentally challenging experiences that I've ever encountered. There were days when I didn't know how I had the strength to get out the bed at 4 a.m. to run miles in the blistering cold and snow. With my knees swollen twice their normal size and arthritis riddled through my body, I know that I completed that program only by the grace of God. I could not have done it alone.

Chapter Four

When I Found My Purpose

My seed of equivalent benefit is that during my time in Shock, I discovered Motivational Speaker/Author Les Brown. Every Tuesday we would go to the library for around 45 minutes. There was a small bookcase with audio cassettes that sat in a corner by themselves. I walked over and began looking through the tapes and came across one entitled "The Courage To Live Your Dreams Vol#2: Powerful Goals A Commitment To Happiness." I grabbed a pair of headphones, popped the tape in, sat down, and began to listen. Les stated that I have Greatness within me. He said, "Goals are like a road map they give you direction, yet many of us just drift along with no goals and no plan for life." He went on to explain that "Happiness is a matter of choice. You can choose to be happy or you can remain stuck in misery. You can choose your happier higher self or a negative lower self. What do you want out of life?" He got me to thinking. What was it that I truly wanted to accomplish in life. He went on and on about the importance of goal setting and how to go about achieving them. Mr. Brown ignited my spirit; I was so intrigued that I wrote down every word he spoke. The time had flown by quickly that day. I was so engaged in what Mr. Brown was saying that I was late falling back in my platoon line. The Drill instructor yelled at me, "Coleman let's go." Needless to say, every Tuesday after that I would run to be the first to grab a cassette player and sit back in the corner of the library feeding my spirit this new soul food that I had recently discovered and loved so much.

LaShaundria Coleman

Before I'd found Les Brown's motivational speeches, I was so empty—my world was very dark and pessimistic, and I had no sense of direction. After feeding my spirit week after week, month after month, I was able to change my mindset, see the light, and realize the Greatness that was truly within me. And I saw that it is my responsibility to cultivate it. Listening to Mr. Brown's messages restored my vision, gave me hope, and inspired me to be and do my personal best. We had a speaker come in to talk to us one day, and it was at that moment I realized that I wanted to be a speaker too. Unfortunately, I don't remember the speaker's name. However, I recall that he delivered a positive message about strength. It wasn't his message that enabled me to come to the realization that I want to speak and help heal hearts and change lives, it was how Mr. Brown's powerful messages were transforming me within and without. It was how my college professors worked to help me begin to change my life.

Listening to those cassette tapes repeatedly had a powerful impact on my life. They helped me to change my mindset, heal my heart, and inspired me to choose my higher self at one of the lowest points in my life. As a mother, it was devastating to be separated away from my child for so long. Hearing Mr. Brown equipped me with the spiritual, mental, and emotional strength I needed to successfully complete the program.

My release date was February 13, 2003. Once I was released, I reunited with my son. It felt so good to be able to hold him, hug him, and kiss his little cheeks. I missed him more than words can ever express. Nonetheless, our bond just reconnected right where it had left off. Post-release I was to serve 5 years on parole. I served some months on parole. One day I went to report for a routine visit and was immediately released from parole. My case fell under the Rockerfella Drug

Law where I was sentenced too harshly. NYS Governor signed the Drug Law Reform Act, which reduced the sentences of nonviolent offenders. I was ecstatic and felt truly blessed to have that burden alleviated from my life. I was determined to operate out of my unlimited ability from that point forward.

Instead of subjecting myself to all of the effects of having been institutionalized. I re-enrolled into college and gained employed at the college at the library as a library assistant in the work study program. I joined organizations and was even elected Vice President of Phi Beta Lambda (Future Business Leaders of America). I completed internships at a New York State Senator's Office and the Buffalo City Hall. I eventually graduated with an Associate's Degree in Business Management. I continued my education at Buffalo State

College where I earned a Bachelor's Degree in Sociology as well. Buffalo State College awarded me with a plaque for providing outstanding community service for the work I performed while interning at The International Institute of Buffalo. After graduation, I continued to volunteer and help in my community. I went on to open up a restaurant on Main Street in Niagara Falls. I named it Mary O's after my grandmother, the late Mary Ollie Smith. We used all her recipes, and all her children worked for me. After my release, I became very involved with my son's schoolwork and extracurricular activities. I enrolled him in baseball, basketball, and a karate program. He played on travel soccer leagues and football as well. I put in massive effort to change my lifestyle to one hundred percent positive. I made a conscious effort to adopt a positive mental attitude. Post-incarceration my primary goal was to give my son a new chance that was much different than the one I had. I did not want to hurt my son again. I kept envisioning the hurt and pain I saw in his eyes and felt when he used to visit me while incarcerated. I didn't ever what him to be subjected to the conditions and environments that I had been subjected to. I didn't want to be separated from him ever again. I had finally matured to the point where I accepted responsibility for my role as a parent and made parenthood my number one priority in life. I valued my relationship with my child more than anything else. It became so important for me to change my lifestyle for him.

My son is my Why. The fact is that as a young black male, he's a target; he's prey in today's society. The fact that I have to pray extra prayers just for his general safety every single day. The fact that statistics says he has a higher chance of going to prison, being murdered or becoming unemployed than making it to age 21 - let alone being successful - is a reality that I deal with. The odds that are against him just for existing as a young African American male are staggering and very disheartening. I always wanted to be an example for him. And to protect and guide him down the most righteous path possible.

My goal is to show him that with faith, hard work, and dedication anything is possible. As long as you are putting forth wholehearted effort to change your life, the universe will reciprocate the rest. I'm showing him that just because your conditions says "no," you have to say "yes" to your success. You have to take ownership of it. You have to make a commitment to not only contend but to win one of the most challenging races that you will ever endure. The race of life.

It will present seemingly insurmountable battles, but you have to always remember what Scripture says:

> You will not have to fight this battle. Take up your positions; stand firm and see the deliverance the LORD will give you, Judah and Jerusalem. Do not be afraid; do not be discouraged. Go out to face them tomorrow, and the LORD will be with you. 2 Chronicles 20:17

My mother is another driving force that encourages me to win. She has been in recovery for over 20 years. Her perseverance to Win no matter what keeps me inspired. She has beaten the odds and continues to display her courage and willpower to this day. We lost my dad in June 2016. He was her soul mate of 35 years. My dad was a provider. He provided whether he had a seven-figure salary, two figure salary or no salary at all.

They worked together to accomplish many great things. My dad is deceased, and I refuse to leave my mom out here alone to fend for herself in today's brutal economy. Ever since my dad passed away, she constantly worries about how she's going to survive solely on survivors benefits. Instead of her being able to focus on living and enjoying the rest of her life, she's burdened with over a million dollars in hospital bills from her deceased husband's cancer treatment. I am determined to place myself in a position where I can take care of my mother and family members. It's upsetting when someone passes away and the family cannot even grieve properly without the additional burden of how they are going to obtain the burial expenses.

My cousin Kalisha's son, Jay, is my motivation as well. Losing her was like losing my sister, the pain I sustained from her passing is indescribable. Kalisha and I had a goal to attend college together. Kalisha never made it to college. In memory of her, I am going to send her son to college to pursue that dream that she never had the opportunity to experience. I know that is the path that she would want him to take. My goal is to pay for her son's college tuition in honor of his mother. I am determined to make that happen for him and her.

It breaks my heart every single time I think about everyone that I lost. I don't want them to have passed away in vain. I want them to know that their passing helped to save me. We used to share our dreams together about being successful. The realization of their absence created a sense of urgency for me to walk in my purpose now because no one is promised later. We are not guaranteed tomorrow; therefore, we truly must seize the moment, the hour, the day. My deceased brother Byron and my Dad believed in me more than I believed in myself at times. I cannot let them down. I cannot let myself down. Jimmie, my one and only son, his life depends on my efforts. I want him to see the over-comer in me and know that he too can overcome any obstacle that life throws in his way. I am not what my past made of me nor are you. I reconstructed my life to become a product of my decisions rather than my upbringing and the conditions and environment around me. I believe that you too can change your life and rise above and beyond any level of success that I have and can attain. You too can change your habits in time to save yourself from a life of ruins. When you're ready to Win, you will put yourself in the game and not only contend, but win. When you decide to achieve victory on any level of your life. It can and shall be done as long as you have principle, positive mental attitude, focus, and the determination to do so. My persistence and determination to change as a result of the pain I sustained continue to fuel me.

Let your pain be a driving force for you to change.

Chapter Five

When

I was blessed with Divine Connections

I operated my restaurant for several years before relocating to Charlotte, North Carolina. I changed my role in life. I changed my mindset, my habits, my circle of friends, my environment, and thus changed my life for the better. I made a conscious effort to not expose myself and my son to any unproductive ways of living. I began expanding my mind by reading my Bible more frequently. I read books and listened to motivational videos and sermons on YouTube. I studied and wrote a lot. I relied heavily on my faith to guide me through the next chapter of my life. When I began to do all of these things, I started to get different results. I began meditating and channeling my energy to a different frequency. I used to say I believed, but I honestly never truly believed in myself or my prayers. Once I started earnestly believing in myself and the requests that I beckoned from the universe, my life began to shift.

Remember the story I shared with you about motivational Speaker/Author Les Brown? Well, fast forward 13 years. Since I've chosen to become a lifelong student, I take great pride in educating myself. I conduct extensive research to find new opportunities, workshops, and training for me to gain knowledge about my area of interest. I was online one day when I came across a flyer advertising a speaker training with none other than Ms. Mamie Brown's baby boy, Mr. Les Brown. I immediately became excited and knew this here was the opportunity for me. I reread the flyer and jotted down the

contact information. I called the number and a woman picked

up. She introduced herself as Dr. Marie Barker. She advised

me that she handles his booking. I expressed my interest in

his upcoming speaker training. She asked me a number of

questions and as I was sharing my story with her, she

interrupted me and said, "Hold on let me see if Les is

available to talk." My heart dropped to my stomach. I said

"Ok." She conferenced Les Brown in on a three-way call and

I was in awe. Les Brown came on the line as his chipper self.

He explained what speaker building tools and techniques he

would be providing at the training. He asked me a few

questions about myself and told Dr. Barker to give me his cell

phone number if I had any further questions before dropping

off the line. I was in such amazement. The fact that I had a

dream to be a speaker and get trained by one of the world's

top motivational speakers and had just hung up the phone

with him was genuinely a blessing. After hanging up the phone, I dropped to my knees and tears began streaming down my face as I shouted my gratitude to God. Shortly thereafter Les Brown called me back. I missed his phone call. He left me a message saying "Hello LaShaundra, LaShaundria, or whateverrrrrrrrrrrr" in that voice he does with his signature laugh. He said, "This is Les Brown calling, give me a call back." Again, I was ecstatic. I called him back as soon as I hung up the voicemail. The phone rang a few times. He picked up. "Les Brown here" I stated my name nervously and he instantly began to talk about the training opportunity. I asked him the cost which might not be a lot to some, but it was to me at the time. He asked me how much does it mean to me to get trained and what type of sacrifice I could make to make it happen. I was sold. Little did he know I was sold when I saw the flyer. I wanted it so bad I could taste it, I saw it, felt it. I tried to make it happen, but I just couldn't within the time-frame. Les didn't know it, but I was homeless at the time, staying with a friend. My belongings were in storage and my son was living with my sister and her family temporarily. I missed that opportunity for training, but it didn't stop me from believing, visualizing, and expecting my training with the legendary Mr. Les Brown. I stayed in faith and continued to attend free training's and workshops in my field of interest.

Two years later, my partner registered us for a free Get Motivated workshop. Les Brown was one of the featured speakers. I felt so blessed and honored to hear him speak live in person. Rewind 13 years ago when I was in prison boot camp at the lowest point in my life. When listening to Les Brown's motivational cassette tapes as encouragement to get through the program, I never imagined myself being trained by him to serve the same purpose 13 years later. God had a plan for me bigger than I had for myself. As is true for you, too.

The day of the workshop I arrived early. I listened to speaker after speaker anticipating Les to take the stage. Something inside of me urged me to call him to ask to meet him in person. I wrestled back and forth with the idea. Finally, I jumped up out of my seat nervously and walked into a quiet part of the venue. I called Les cell phone. It rang twice, and he picked up. He answered, "Hello this is Les." I stated "Hello Mr. Brown, my name is LaShaundria Coleman. I spoke with you on the threeway with Dr. Barker a few years ago. I'm calling you because I'm at the event you're going to be speaking at today and I was wondering would it be possible to meet you in person?" Without hesitation he said, "Yes, I can meet you in person, my flight arrives in Charlotte at 2 p.m. I get to the venue at 3 p.m. call me and I'll bring you backstage." I said, "Thank you so much, Mr. Brown; I look forward to meeting you" and hung up the phone. When I entered back into the room and walked back to my seat, it took everything I had not to shout out with excitement I'm going backstage to meet with Mr. Brown. I just chuckled as I told my partner and brother in law.

I kept looking at my watch until 3 p.m. arrived. I called Mr. Brown and he advised me where to go to meet him backstage. He was standing in a general area when I walked up to him introduced myself and hugged him. I introduced the people I was with as well. He invited us to his green room to chat with him. He asked me what do I want to do with my life. I told him that I would like to be a speaker and help to transform lives like he does. He dropped a few jewels on me before someone peeked their head in and told him they were ready for him to go on. We hugged and I went out and watched him speak. I saw him in a much more down to earth light. Mr. Brown is one of the most genuinely generous persons that I have ever met. He's so compassionate and committed to sharing his message of change and resilience. His honest effort to train and develop the mindsets of hundreds of thousands of people is astonishing.

Later that day I received a phone call from Mr. Brown. He asked me what parts of his presentation I liked the most? I replied, "The part where you were extremely persistent at the radio station. You just kept going back every day until they eventually hired you." We laughed, he then invited me to a speaker training in Orlando, Florida. Once he disclosed the cost of the training I could have become discouraged and not said anything or just tried to negotiate the fee to what was feasible for me. I said, "Mr. Brown, I don't have that much money." It wasn't a lot either because his training are invaluable, but it was just a lot for me at the time. He said, "This is what I'm going to do for you, what can you come up with?" I gave him an amount he said, "Ok, call Calvin at this number. Tell him I said this and he'll take care of you." I was on the other end of the phone smiling, crying, jumping, heart beating fast, going through all sorts of emotions. I thanked Mr. Brown repeatedly. Called Calvin, flew out to Orlando, Florida, to the Shenandoah Valley Resort and Spa for the I Have To Speak Training. I met up with Mr. Les Brown again and told him a little about my story. He said I remind him of Peewee

Herman always dressed up all colorful. We laughed and the rest is history. The moral of that story is to never give up on your goals and dreams. Cultivate your dreams until they become your reality. Anything is possible. As Muhammad Ali said: "If my mind can conceive it, and my heart can believe it, then I can achieve it."

The reality of Mr. Brown writing my Foreword for this book is confirmation that When you make a conscious effort to change your life and you work at it every single day over a period of time, you will Win the results you envision. Life has taught me that my ability to learn from defeat is essential to me winning. The greatest lesson I learned is that I cannot be beaten and that failure is a necessary component of success. As my mentor says, "You have to fail your way to success!" So don't let your fear of failure prevent you from succeeding.

I've been disqualified in life plenty of times, but I didn't let that stop me from competing and doing what I was meant to do. I am determined to get to that next level in life for my son, my mother, sisters, brothers, cousins, friends, and even strangers. I do this for you, too. My destiny is to be a messenger. It took me a long time to figure it out, but I am thankful that I finally came to the realization that my purpose is to serve, to inspire, and to motivate people to keep pushing forward in spite of their circumstances. My life serves as a testimony of God's grace, God's goodness and mercy. Had I not experienced all that I did, I would not be able to provide you with advice based on actual experience.

Through experience, I have learned that we truly do create the exact amount of success or failure that we have. Once you are able to own up to that fact, you will immediately start to take control of your life. You will begin to visualize what your life can look like and begin to create that vision; it will manifest itself as long as you are consistent and committed to pursuing your greatness. I learned that as long as we give our maximum effort to the race, we have just as much of a chance of winning as anyone else.

We are more than conquerors. We don't have to live up to society's expectation of who we should be based on the experiences that we encountered. The battle is already won. If we fall down, we just have to get up dust ourselves off and keep moving forward. You will eventually arrive at your desired destination as long as you never give up and continue racing towards it. I kept running despite my physical condition and the doctor telling me not to run. I kept going despite my past, despite my race and socioeconomic background, despite coming from a broken home, despite being a junior high school dropout, despite my criminal record, despite my lifestyle choices, despite all the odds I faced and the lack of means I had to reach my goals, I continued to press forward. All my life I've been told that I cannot and will not succeed. I am here to show you that anything is possible and yes I have and will continue to Win. And not only will I Win, but I will also show a multitude of individuals how to Win as well when positive changes are made in their lives. The sky is not the limit, as long as there is infinite space in space, there are truly no limitations in life.

Chapter Six

Win

The will to win, the desire to succeed, the urge to reach your full potential... these are the keys that will unlock the door to personal excellence.
~Confucius

Winning represents many things. When I speak of winning, I'm referring to a spiritual state, mental, emotional, physical, and financial as well. For me, I am winning when I am living in alignment with God's laws. I am winning when I am surrounded by healthy relationships. I am winning when I am happy and Blessed enough to be able to help others. I am winning when I am able to share life changing information with my family members and new people I meet. Winning is not just about gaining a victory in a contest or conflict.

Winning is a way of life, a state of mind. It's an attitude and a spirit that is innately within you. You just have to manifest it, call it forth, and cultivate it.

The objective of The When|Win Approach is to help bring forth the inner winner in you when you make a solid decision to create positive change and aggressively pursue your goals and dreams. These are the principles and strategies I applied to help me overcome challenges in my life to achieve my desired level of success. The winning Principles are a conscious and disciplined routine commitment to productive activities that I consistently practice. Persistence and determination enabled me to create my desired winning lifestyle. Taking swift action with the aforementioned factors will assist you in creating a winning attitude and lifestyle for yourself as well.

The When|Win Approach is not a "fix my life overnight" type fix. This is not a book of unproven theories. These are my actual experiences and experiences that other thought leaders have encountered throughout our lives to produce positive change. These are actual steps I have taken to create positive results in my life. Constantly declare that you are a Winner, that is the mindset that you have to possess. Winning is the principle that you have to operate on. When you have a strong burning desire to succeed, to be your absolute best in every area of your life, then and only then will you strive to pursue the greatness that is within you. I've learned that I have to want it for myself. It doesn't matter how badly someone else wants you to be successful; you have to want it for you. When you put forth 100% plus effort to be your best in all that you do, then the efforts of your 100% plus will be reciprocated back to you.

You will Win the game of life when you understand that life is a series of constant challenges designed to bring forth the inner winner in you. Don't quit and never give up no matter how challenging situations may get. Know that whatever you're going through is part of the journey. You have to encounter setbacks, disappointments, and failure in order to win. No successful person has ever reached their level of success by not experiencing any challenges. Successful people obtained their levels of success because they successfully overcame all the challenges, setbacks, and temporary defeats that they experienced. The ability to learn from defeat is an essential principle of success.

As a baby is learning to walk and falls down hundreds of times, never once does it cross their minds to give up and quit trying. We are born with the confidence and ambition that we need to be natural winners. From infancy, the experiences that we encounter in life either build us up or strip us of our winning spirit. In today's society, there are an overwhelming amount of discouraging factors that contribute to the average person being discouraged on an everyday basis. The When|Win Approach is a tool that I encourage you to use to assist in the process of learning, growing, solving problems, staying motivated, inspired, and remaining focused on your goals and dreams.

The When| Win Approach allows you to reflect on your current attitude and behaviors so that you may learn new information, ideas, skills, and practices to create a more enjoyable lifestyle. When you want to do something, you have to sit back and think realistically about what steps do you need to take to get the job done. For instance, let's say your goal is to meet your favorite mainstream recording artist; however, you are from a small city and the mainstream artist rarely even visits your city to perform. You have to think realistically, what do I have to do to align myself with the opportunity? Most individuals would sit back hoping to just magically meet this person as opposed to putting themselves in a better-suited position to make the dream become a reality. There are a lot of avenues one could take to put themselves in a better position. For instance, if the artist is scheduled for an upcoming tour stop in the next closest city, you can invest in backstage passes or invest in meet and greet options if available. You can buy front row tickets to better position yourself to be seen by the artist. The fact of the matter is that

72

you have to invest in your dreams. If you are not willing to invest in your dream, it is nothing more than a wish. When I say invest in your dream, I mean you have to put forth time, effort, resources, and a lot of sweat equity to bring it to fruition.

When I stopped allowing negative outside forces to dictate how I feel on the inside, that was when I won the power to control how I felt and took action in my life. When you realize that you are in control of how you feel on the inside, then you will harness your powers effectively and no one can control your emotions from the outside. When you learn how to control your emotions, you will respond as opposed to reacting and giving yourself leverage over your opposition. I encourage you to equip yourself with these When|Win quotes as they serve to strengthen you and will help you to stay focused, inspired, and motivated while heading in a new and positive direction in life.

Chapter Seven

When|Win

One of the Greatest lessons I learned in life is When I realized that I can Win. When I realized through temporary defeat that I cannot be beat.

When: You understand success principles
Win: You will gain the ability to succeed from defeat

When: You let go of who you currently are
Win: You gain the ability to become someone a lot greater

When: You understand the value of time
Win: You will learn how to use it to serve you

When: You understand the importance of finishing
Win: You will gain the courage to get started

When: You understand the importance of the win
Win: You will gain the ability to contend

When: You create a plan to be prosperous
Win: You will position yourself to gain prosperity

When: You practice for years in private
Win: You will win in public

When: You stop making excuses and start making progress
Win: You will begin to experience positive results that are
beneficial to you

When: You stop feeling powerless and realize that you have
infinite energy within you
Win: You will begin to feel powerful and use your strength to
serve yourself and others.

When: You stop fearing the loss of your job
Win: You will gain the focus and confidence you need to
perform the job task effectively and efficiently

When: You make a conscious effort to stop complaining
about your job

Win: You will begin to use your energy and time to find a new job, go into business for yourself or design an employment plan that will give you a peace of mind and the happiness that you desire

When: You make a choice to get started
Win: You will place yourself on a path to create your own success

When: You stop putting things off until tomorrow
Win: You will acquire the understanding and importance of completing the task today

When: The battle is difficult
Win: The victory will come easily

When: You believe in your vision
Win: You will see your vision come to fruition

When: You expand your circle of influence
Win: You will position yourself to acquire new opportunities

When: You wake up and work on your dream daily
Win: Your dream will become a reality

When: You never give up on your dream
Win: You will see your desired end result come to pass

When: You stop living someone else vision for your life
Win: You will gain the ability to see and live your own vision
for your life

When: You make a different choice
Win: You will achieve a different result

When: You change your thinking from thoughts of lack
Win: You will acquire thoughts of abundance

When: You stay focused
Win: You will achieve your goals

When: You stop focusing on what you don't have
Win: You will gain the ability to focus on what you do have
and use it to your advantage

When: You replace your negative thoughts with positive
thoughts
Win: You will begin to have more positive results in your life

When: You are patient
Win: You will receive blessings at the right time

When: You don't give up on yourself
Win: You put yourself in alignment to be victorious

When: Your life is shaped by positive thoughts
Win: You will become what you think

When: You are loving, honest, loyal, and true in all that you do
Win: All of the above will be reciprocated to you

When: You stop concentrating on the idea of people loving you
Win: You will gain the strength to focus on loving yourself

When: You show gratitude
Win: You will attract more

When: You are not satisfied with mediocre
Win: You gain the ability to turn ordinary into extraordinary

When: You stop wishing
Win: You will gain the strength to start doing

When: You stop thinking small and start to think big
Win: You will achieve big results

When: You believe
Win: You will receive

When: You ask
Win: You will receive

When: You know what questions to ask
Win: You will gain the knowledge of how to apply the answers to your life

When: You let go of what should of or could have happened
Win: You will gain the ability to live with what did or is happening

When: You stop jumping from one thing to the next and concentrate on one project at a time
Win: You will gain the ability to follow through

When: You change your mind from negative thoughts
Win: You will change the experiences that you're encountering in life to positive ones

When: You stop looking to others for approval
Win: You will gain the approval of yourself

When: You step up in life
Win: You gain the ability to raise your standards

When: You realize and accept the fact that you are God's masterpiece and that you have a divine purpose
Win: You will acquire the confidence and strength to walk in your divine purpose

When: You truly have love for self
Win: You will gain the power to not look to others for validation or acceptance

When: You open yourself up
Win: You will put yourself into alignment to experience endless possibilities

When: You believe that it can be done
Win: You will achieve the strength to do it

When: You acknowledge and accept your responsibilities
Win: You gain the maturity to take care of them

When: You decide to take action
Win:You will gain the ability to overcome obstacles and challenges that are in your path

When: You stop thinking about it
Win: You will gain the ability to take action

When: You stop complaining
Win: You start gaining the strength, knowledge, and energy
you need to get the job done

When: You stop comparing yourself to others
Win: You will be able to see the value in yourself

When: You cease to make excuses
Win: You will use your power to make a way/ make it
happen

When: You put an end to living a life by chance
Win: You will win the ability to live the life of your choice
and begin to step into your destiny

When: You embrace your individuality
Win: You will acquire the courage to operate free of social
constraints

When: You pick your head up and realize how close you are
to the achieving your goal
Win: You will gain the strength to finish the race

When: You give without expecting anything in return
Win: You will gain the ability to feel more fulfilled

When: You realize that you are empowered
Win: You will gain the ability to make what you thought to be impossible possible

When: You accept responsibility to do what you have to do
Win: You achieve what you are destined to achieve

When: You become who you are destined to become
Win: You will gain the ability to positively impact your life

When: You are confident
Win: You gain the strength to not be affected by the opinion of others

When: You love and accept yourself
Win: You will gain the "I was born to stand out not to fit in" mentality

When: You start using your leverage
Win: You will gain the ability to do more with less.

When: You push yourself
Win: You acquire the courage to rise above your fears

When: You change your negative behaviors
Win: You will gain the ability to develop more positive behaviors

When: You stop lying to yourself
Win: You will gain the ability to walk in truth

When: You put together a recipe for success
Win: You'll gain the skill to cook it and make it taste good

When: You put an end to living a life by chance
Win: You will gain the ability to live the life of your choice

When: You cease to make excuses
Win: You acquire the strength to make the necessary changes
in your life

When: You understand the fact that you are and halt being
used
Win :You will gain the realization that you are and find new
ways to become useful

When: You end a relationship where you are being
manipulated
Win: You'll gain the courage to take your power back so that
you will be liberated

When: You stop competing against yourself and others
Win: You will enable yourself to be victorious

When: You stop being a victim
Win: You will use your power to be a victor

When: You stop following others
Win: You will gain the ability to follow your own intuition

When: You stop focusing on the burden
Win: You will gain the ability to focus on your blessings

When: You stop focusing on what you want
Win: You will gain the knowledge to obtain what you need

When: You exercise regularly
Win: You will gain the strength to start to feel better about yourself, and it will boost your confidence

When: You stop underestimating yourself and give it everything you've got 100% of the time
Win: You will gain the ability to create a winning culture for your life 100% of the time

When: You stop hanging around your friends who are not successful and start to aggressively pursue success
Win: You will gain new relationships and networks of people that can help accelerate you to the next level in your life

When: You accept the things that can't be changed
Win: You will gain the strength to make positive changes to the areas that you can change in your life

When: You refrain from indulging in self-destructive habits and non-beneficial routines.
Win: You will acquire the ability to allow yourself the opportunity to produce positive results and benefit from routines and habits that add value to your life

When: You stop acting out irrationally
Win: You will gain the ability to have more influence over a positive outcome

When: You learn how to delegate tasks
Win: You will gain the ability to save yourself valuable time and energy.

When: You are conscious of your time management
Win: You will gain the ability to become more organized and reduce your stress

When: You exercise your independence
Win: You will gain the ability to not rely on others

When: You outgrow the capacity to go where you're tolerated
Win: You will gain the knowledge of only going where you're celebrated

When: You stop engaging in lustful behaviors
Win: You will allow yourself the opportunity to gain real love

When: You cease to make excuses
Win: You acquire the strength to make necessary changes in your life

When: You put a halt to being used
Win: You will gain the ability to become a resource to yourself first and foremost

When: You love yourself
Win: You will win the love, admiration, and respect of others

When: You seek knowledge
Win: You will acquire the tools needed to take you where you want to go in life

When: You stop being complacent

Win: You will gain the knowledge needed to change your situation

When: You truly believe that faith can move mountains
Win: You will gain the strength to overcome challenges in your life

When: You are open minded
Win:You will gain the ability to see the bigger picture

When: You stretch your thoughts
Win: You win gain the strength to execute them

When: You let go of your past
Win: You will gain the ability to visualize a better future for yourself

When: You stop complaining about your problems
Win: You will gain the ability to use your energy to find a resolution

When: You Prepare (Practice)
Win: You will gain more confidence

When: You live your dreams
Win: You will leave this earth with awesome memories

When: You allow yourself to see what is not visible
Win: You will achieve what you thought was not possible

When: You become a good listener
Win: You gain the ability to better understand others

When: You talk less
Win: You will begin to do more

When: You work hard
Win: You will be rewarded for your hard work..Stay focused!!

When: You are a continual learner
Win: You position yourself to be exposed to new information, tools, and opportunities for advancement

When: You respond less to negativity
Win: You will gain more peace

When: You stop focusing on who is rooting for you or not
Win: You will gain the ability to pursue your goals and dreams nonstop

When: You make a choice to take a chance
Win: Your life will change

When: You think big
Win: You widen your perspective

When: You stop waiting for the New Year to make resolutions
Win: You will learn how to use the 365 days annually to work on your personal development, create new opportunities and reach your goals. Ex. If you set one new goal per week, you will accomplish 52 goals per year

You will Win "Not If" but When you make a conscious decision to contend and give the race of life your maximum effort. It is not a matter of if you can win, it is a matter of when you change the current conditions of your life to gain victory spiritually, mentally, physically, emotionally and financially.

Let me be clear: There is not one winner on this planet earth that did not encounter a lot of failure before reaching their high levels of achievement. I learned that fear and failure are natural parts of life; however, we don't have to allow them to control us. I've faced a lot of scary situations all throughout my life, and the best advice that I can give you is to face it.

Don't go around it, don't act like it doesn't exist, face your fears head on. I remember when I used to feel nervous about going to a new school or meeting new people. I made up all of these negative thoughts about what could or would possibly happen. I used to over-think the situation and send myself into an internal panic. As I got older, I began to realize that I had a lot of self-defeating thoughts that were causing me to have these feelings. We should not expect the worst outcome. Thoughts are things. We have to be extremely careful of what we think and say so that we don't weaken our spirits. Think positive thoughts in an effort to receive positive results.

I refused to allow the darkness of my past to dictate my future. No shame, regret or guilt would hold me emotionally in bondage. I chose to thrive, I chose to let go and free myself and walk in the light. No worry, stress, discouragement or temporary defeat would interfere with my desire to become successful. I overcame all of life's challenges by the elimination of fear.

Possessing a winning mentality is powerful. My body has limitations. However, my mind does not have any limitations. I knew that my strength was not at the physical level, so I dominated the mental level. I used my brain to think myself into becoming successful. I prepared myself mentally to achieve my goals. You can do the same as well. Get your mind in the game! You still have a chance to Win.

Chapter Eight

Winning Principles

Principles govern our lives and are constant. The principles you choose to operate your life on are a major key to you either winning or losing in life. I witnessed a lot of change in my life by relying on my underlying principles. The principles that you operate on will transcend through your daily attitudes, habits, and actions. Your behavior reflects your principles or lack thereof. Allow your principles to control your actions.

Below you will find a list of 7 Principles that were instrumental in changing my life. I labeled them the 7 Winning Principles. These are the principles that I applied to my daily life, which guided me to the creation of my winning lifestyle and can do the same for you if applied consistently.

I encourage you to set forth guiding principles to follow so that your life will go in the right direction and to increase your chances of happiness, positiveness, and success. Principles represent the values and fundamental norms that govern a person, organization, business or group.

The power of the 7 Winning principles is in the application. Applied these principles teach you what is desirable versus undesirable. As well as how to overcome challenges and achieve and ensure success in all areas of your life.

Chapter Nine

Winning Principle #1
Awareness

By taking the time to stop and appreciate who you are and what you've achieved - and perhaps learned through a few mistakes, stumbles and losses - you actually can enhance everything about you. Self-acknowledgment and appreciation are what give you the insights and awareness to move forward toward higher goals and accomplishments.

~Jack Canfield

1. Awareness- The first element of change

Consciousness of a situation or fact was one of the first changes that had to take place in order for me to create positive change in my life. The ability to be cognizant of what you know, feel, believe and were taught will enable you to organize decisions and information more effectively.

I encourage you to conduct an honest self-evaluation to analyze the space that you are currently occupying in life. It is important to take a self-evaluation so that we prepare ourselves to take personal responsibility for our own choices and life. When we understand that our life is a direct product of the choices we make as individuals, we won't feel the need to blame others for the results of our life.

When you have knowledge of a situation or fact, you can be better equipped to handle it. Applying the principle of Awareness in your life will give you a vantage point instead of remaining unaware. I feel as though once you are aware of who you are, what you want, how you are going to obtain it and most importantly why it is important to you, then you will proactively do what it takes to create your desired results and lifestyle.

For me, awareness was the first step in creating a triumphant lifestyle. I had to take an honest look at myself and my life to determine if I liked what I saw? Was I satisfied with my home life, work life, my relationships and social life? Did I feel that changes could be made to help improve my situation? I had to become consciously aware of and accept my strengths and weaknesses and the things that I could change versus things that I could not. Things I could not change like the weather, my physical deformities, my past, etc. Taking this self-evaluation helped me to realize that there is always room for improvement. No one has a perfect life.

I was able to produce positive change by letting go. **When:** you let go of who you currently are **Win:** You gain the ability to become someone a lot greater. Once you accept the things you cannot change and take massive action towards changing the things that you can, you will notice positive changes occurring in your life.

It is important to be aware of the level of consciousness that you operate in. Speaker Jim Rohn said it best, "You are the average of the five people you spend the most time with." You develop habits and behaviors as those of the five people that you occupy a majority of your time with. I urge you to be extremely cautious of the company that you keep. I had to truly evaluate the individuals I surrounded myself with. I had to ask myself, are these people adding value to my life or taking withdrawals from my life? Or are they simply there just existing doing neither just in the way. I came to the realization that you have to change your immediate environment if you want to change yourself and your life.

Our interactions are influenced by the people we surround ourselves around. So, therefore it is imperative to be selective of the company you keep as the company you keep has the potential to influence your situation. When we surround ourselves with individuals that are negative minded, they tend to give us poor advice and further perpetuate negative situations. People that are positive minded tend to provide advice that can potentially elevate us.

Life demands a high level of awareness. I've found that it costs me less in the long run to just pay attention upfront and to be aware of the space I'm occupying in life. You pay a bigger price for not being aware or attentive to important matters in your life. A level of consciousness is a state where an individual emotion penetrates all awareness. Be aware of your natural instinct. Be aware of who you are and what you desire from life. When we operate from a higher level of consciousness, we get better results in life.

The level of consciousness you operate in affects your personal experiences and behaviors. When you reach higher levels of consciousness in your life, your perception will change. You will be calmer in your thinking and decision-making process. Lower levels of consciousness produce emotions of anger, fear, guilt, despair, and pride.

Once you become aware of the situation, focus your attention steadily towards a central objective to fix the matter. Engage in focused thinking. Focused thinking will limit the amount of clutter and distractions that you allow into your mind. In doing so, you allow yourself better concentration and have clarity of thoughts. The book "How Successful People Think" by Author John C. Maxwell teaches that focused thinking will bring positive energy and power to almost any situation.

Selective focused thinking will allow you to identify what your priorities are, have clear goals, time to develop ideas, time to cultivate your dreams, and will take you to the next level. I recommend you to limit the number of distractions that you are allowing into your life and carve out time for focused thinking. Concentrating on items of focus will allow you to manage all your daily affairs. Writing down the information that you are focusing on and keeping it in front of you each day will allow you to concentrate on what matters.

It is extremely important to be aware of your emotional state during personal and interpersonal relationships as well. Having emotional intelligence plays a major role in your professional and personal success. I had to learn how to respond versus react to situations in life. I was unaware of the level of emotional intelligence that I was displaying until my former manager brought it to my attention. Several years ago,

I used to go to work stressed out as a result of my brother being in passing. I held my emotions inside; I did not share my personal life and situations that I was experiencing at my place of employment; however, it showed. I used to arrive at work unlike my usual self, snappy and very disconnected from the job I was performing. Once my emotional distress began to show up in my work, my manager pulled me to the side and said: "I don't know what you are going through, but I know it's something because you are not your usual self nor are you performing at your best ability." I explained that I was on edge because of my brother's health concerns. He explained to me that he had been through some unpleasant situations recently as well and he read a book that shifted his emotional state from a state of indifference to a state of emotional control. He gave me a book to read. The title of the book was "Emotional Intelligence 2.0." Reading that book helped me to realize that I was not managing my emotions effectively. I was very impulsive with my emotions and I lacked thoughtfulness in my responses. You must possess the ability to shift your thoughts and emotions. I was reacting to every situation as opposed to responding. It is essential to know when to bring the elevator back down to the lobby from the penthouse. Every situation cannot and should not be escalated. When I was younger, I used to be flip mode status. I use to switch on and off quicker than a light switch. Nowadays I use strategies such as counting to ten seven times and breathing exercises to help me maintain or even regain my self-control. Reducing my intake of caffeine and sugars helped me to manage my adrenaline from running over and controlling my behaviors as well. By practicing the use of control over my emotions allowed me to think more rationally.

Having awareness is essential to your ability to create positive change in your life. As my mentor, Les Brown states, "You can't see the picture when you're in the frame." So it is important to have an open mind and value outside perspectives. And to step outside the frame to see things from different views in efforts to arrive at a different perspective.

Chapter Ten

Winning Principle #2
Ask

"Ask for what you want and be prepared to get it!"
~Maya Angelou

2. Ask- It is important to be specific when asking our higher

power for what I desire from life.

Scripture says, "Ask and it will be given to you; seek and you

will find; knock and the door will be opened to you" Matthew

7:7. It is true that a closed mouth doesn't get fed. We have to

make bold, specific prayer request to our higher power and

our universe. Scripture also says that "The prayer of a

righteous person is powerful and effective" (James 5:16). I've

bared witness to this truth. You cannot be scared to ask for what you want. We cannot be fearful or doubtful. We must approach the situation with great confidence so that our higher power will respond as we desire.

A lot of times we go through life silent, meek, and timid. We act shy and embarrassed around others. Even when we pray, we whisper in secrecy. For some reason or another something that happened in our lives discouraged us from using our voice. Something or someone sent a message that was loud and clear that said we don't have the right to speak up or ask our universe for what we want boldly. I encourage you to unlearn what you were taught in that area and try this new way of thinking and living. Ask and you shall receive. The universe is not rendering any results for you because you are not deliberately summoning anything.

I've found that there is absolute power in calling forth what we want. I believe in the law of attraction. Like truly attracts like. We are responsible for the positive or negative energy that we allow in our lives. I use my energy to think optimistically about whatever it is I'm facing good, bad or indifferent. You too can do the same. Be mindful of the thoughts that you are thinking. Harness only positive thoughts so that those positive visions will come to fruition in the coming days, weeks or months. Acknowledge the negative thoughts that you are having so you can combat them with positive new visions.

I used visualization and positive self-affirmation techniques to help change my life. I spend 20-30 minutes per day - sometimes more - visualizing about what I want out of life and how exactly I am going to go about getting it. I'll share a true story with you about the power of asking and visualization and how I witnessed it work in my life. Back in 2011, I moved to Charlotte, North Carolina. I was driving a 2009 Pontiac Rendezvous at the time. It wasn't in the best condition, but it drove. I didn't drive it to Charlotte though. I pulled it with my u-haul because I feared that it would not have made it.

I used to have to drive over 15 miles daily to get back and forth from work. Sometimes my truck would start; sometimes it wouldn't. I was so tired of worrying and stressing what could happen. I had recently discovered the movie, "The Secret." That day I made a conscious decision to apply the principles that I had learned to my life. And not only to apply them but to believe it. Every single day on my way to and from work, I would rub the center of my steering wheel in the pattern of the Mercedes-Benz emblem. I used to say "Thank you God for Blessing Me with this Mercedes Benz." "Thank you, God, for Blessing me with this Mercedes Benz." At the time I didn't have a Mercedes-Benz; I was driving my little old beat up Pontiac Buick Rendezvous. I was just activating my faith by asking God and visualizing and thanking God in advance for the blessing I was expecting to receive.

A year later, my truck was on its last leg. The number of times per week it cut off on me increased dramatically. I had been to a few other dealerships in the days prior. I did not find anything that suited me. I prayed and prayed and prayed that my car would make it to the Mercedes-Benz dealership and in between the prayer, I was thanking God for the new car I would receive once I got there. My truck literally slid into a parking space in the front of the establishment. I prayed some more before I went in. I was in a far worse position financially. My credit score was a 424 at the time. All I had was faith and a few dollars and a beat up trade in. I went into a certified Mercedes-Benz dealership as if I belonged there and my credit score was an 800. Apparently, I did belong there because I was there. In the words of the great Les Brown, "I'm not telling you about this to impress you. However, I'm sharing my story with you to impress upon you that anything is possible." I walked in that dealership with great faith and the confidence of David when he set out to fight Goliath. I believed that the win was mine before I was approved for my new Mercedes-Benz Benz C230. Me hearing the words of my approval was just confirmation.

I built a good relationship with a representative by the name of Bob. It was Bob's first day back to work, at the end of the month and end of the quarter. Needless to say, Bob worked extra hard to make it a Win/win for the both of us. A lot of pessimism would argue that the aforementioned factors influenced my chances of approval. I would argue that yes those were small factors that influenced my approval chances. However, I was already pre-approved by the most high. The fact that I had even decided to go to that specific Mercedes-Benz dealership was ordained. The fact that I have this here testimony further validates my claim that it was ordained.

Our universe has a special way of delivering what we ask for. I believe that I acquired my desires simply because I asked. We have the ability to manifest anything we want. **When:** You ask and believe. **Win:** You will receive!

Chapter Eleven

Winning Principle #3
Believe

"You have to believe in yourself when no one else does that
makes you a winner right there"
~Venus Williams

3. Believe - You have to have a belief in yourself that's rock

solid. No matter what happens to you, your faith will not be

moved.

The belief that you have in yourself is vital to your success

and overall way of life. You have to believe in you first and

foremost. You cannot expect anyone else to believe in you if

you don't believe in yourself wholeheartedly. You have to

112

have an unapologetic faith and confidence that you are who you say you are. That you will do all the things, you said you will do. And that you will be everything our higher power put in your heart to be. Scripture says, "Therefore I tell you, whatever you ask for in prayer, believe that you have received it, and it will be yours." Mark 11:24. You have to believe it.

When you believe in yourself it won't matter who don't believe in you; you won't have time to focus on naysayers and nonbelievers because you are too busy believing in yourself, doing you, cultivating your dreams while focusing on your goals.

Belief can be used interchangeably with faith. Faith is described as the act of having complete confidence and trust in something or someone. As with belief, faith requires us to put trust in things that we cannot see in the physical. It forces us to rely on our spiritual and mental strength to guide us through our trials. You have to believe in what you are summoning without any doubt whatsoever. One ounce of doubt will cancel everything out.

You have to intentionally rid yourself of doubt and disbelief. Allow yourself to release the things that you have been conditioned to believe. I want you to do this, start believing that you are capable of accomplishing your goals and dreams because it is possible for you to do so. You are capable of passing that test, you are capable of making that team, you are capable of standing up to that bully, you are capable of losing weight, you are capable of becoming healthy, you are capable of escaping that abusive and toxic relationship, you are capable of getting through your divorce, you are capable of falling in love again, you are capable of beating that addiction, you are capable of having financial abundance, you are capable of not becoming a repeat offender, you are capable of turning your life around, you are capable of making a difference in this world, and you are capable of overcoming any challenge that life throws your way. Believe in yourself during both calm and challenging times, let your beliefs be unwavering.

Limit the amount of negative self talk. We can be our own worst critic at times. It is extremely important to make it a daily routine to speak positive self-affirmations. I found strength looking in the mirror affirming who I am and thanking God in advance for what I expected.

It is important that you refrain from negative self talk. A Lot of us talk negatively about ourselves consciously as well as unconsciously. It is never okay to put yourself down. It is never okay to insult ourselves whether we are joking or serious because words are very powerful. Scripture says, "Death and life are in the power of the tongue" Proverbs 18:21. It is crucial to our personal development and growth to only speak life unto ourselves and others. As my mentor, Les Brown, says, "Thou shall decree a thing and it shall be established unto you." Do not give your power to negative self talk. Use your energy to only talk about and declare positive self-serving thoughts. We have to be our own cheerleader first and foremost. You can rid your life of negativity by constantly reciting positive talk and having a positive outlook. And not only possessing these qualities but also believing wholeheartedly in these qualities as well.

We must be conscious of the thoughts that we believe and words that we speak. Especially when dealing with our children. Our children are very impressionable, and it is vital that we instill the most righteous belief system and principles in them. If we are constantly yelling at our children, discouraging them, telling them negative things out of anger, then that seed will germinate in them. They will become angry, believe what you tell them, and walk through life discouraged and defeated. Our words can either bless our children or curse our children. Bless our house or curse our house. Proverbs 15:4 says that a soothing tongue is a tree of life, but a perverse tongue crushes the spirit. Scripture says that we should "Train up a child in the way that he should go, and when he is older he will not depart from it."

Other than the Holy Bible, one of the most powerful books that I read in reference to using the power of words effectively was "The Power of I Am" by Joel Olsteen. That book transformed my belief system about those two Powerful Words. Those two words not only changed my belief system, but they also helped me to realize how powerful I truly am. By studying the power of I Am, I was able to apply those concepts to my life, and in doing so it thrust me into positions I had only imagined, but in a shorter period of time than I had expected. I highly recommend you read that book too so that it will empower you as well as provide you with additional strategies that focus on speaking blessing over your life. As Joel says, "what follows your I Am's will come looking for you." For instance, if you are constantly stating that you are broke, you will attract brokenness. Instead of saying that you are broke, say "I Am conquering a financial challenge right now." If you are saying you can't do something, you will attract more defeat. Instead of saying you can't do something say, "I am learning new ways to overcome this obstacle." Always speak and declare things the way that you want to see them, not the way that they are. Whether it's a conversation with yourself or others always put a positive spin on your negative thoughts and conversation.

My life began to change dramatically when I began to operate in a spirit of expectancy. Not only did I have to have awareness, ask and believe. I had to expect what I was summoning. When you live in expectancy, it brings you closer to your dreams and goals coming to pass. You must operate in a spirit of expectancy; however, you must put your trust in God's timing. God will allow your prayers to come to pass at the appointed date and time. You can expect to receive your blessing. However, you must have patience as well.

The story that I shared with you in chapter three illustrates the power of belief and faith. I learned a very memorable lesson from that experience. Had I just believed and followed through with what I said I was going to do, I would not have received my second felony conviction. I made a commitment to myself to no longer involve myself with that at-risk lifestyle. Because of my lack of belief my lack of faith, I received a phone call from an old acquaintance and fell victim to temptation. I encourage you to believe wholeheartedly, stay patient, stay faithful, and you will see your desired end result come to pass.

He replied, "Because you have so little faith. Truly I tell you, if you have faith as small as a mustard seed, you can say to this mountain, 'Move from here to there,' and it will move. Nothing will be impossible for you." Matthew 17:20

"Fear and faith cannot reside at the under the same roof; one must be evicted" ~**LaShaundria Coleman**

Chapter Twelve

Winning Principle #4
Commitment

"Most people fail, not because of lack of desire, but, because lack of commitment"
~Vince Lombardi

4.Commitment - The ability to do what you should do even when you don't feel like doing it is the type of discipline that is required for success.

The first step in making a commitment is to decide that this is what you are going to do. You have to make a decision that you are going to be committed. The first major commitment was to my higher power. God will not bless a situation that you are not committed to. Making a commitment is essential in the process of change. I started to see positive changes in my life once I began to make decisions and commit to what I had decided. Not only did I begin to make tough decisions and commit to doing what I had decided, but I also acted on it. I had to take action.

Commitment is where you are fully devoted to the cause whether or not it was very challenging or did not present a challenge. When you commit to something, you will see that thing come to pass. When you are committed, you're not doing it because you're being told to or reminded to. You do it because you are fully devoted and 100 percent dedicated to accomplishing what you set forth to do. If you are not committed to anything, you will give up easily on things. When we are not as far as we think we should be with a task or in life in general, we tend to blame the devil, haters and other people for our woes. When in fact, our own lack of commitment is a primary factor in our lack of progress.

I've learned that you not only have to be at the right place at the right time in life, but you also have to be the right person asking the right questions as well. When you are committed to taking a proactive approach to your attainment of success in life, when you are committed to being a continual learner, when you are committed to doing whatever it takes to make positive changes in your life, when you are committed and not just interested in taking your life to that next level. Then and only then will you experience a changed mindset, habits, and lifestyle.

I made a commitment to put my all into changing my lifestyle. This book is an example of my commitment to my dream. I believed in myself, and because of my self-belief, others poured into my dream as well. If you are not committed to your dream, don't expect others to be committed to your dream. If you do not invest in your dream, don't expect others to invest in your dream. It all begins and ends with you. With the exception of the universal force. You determine what direction your life is going to go in. The pen is in your hand. You can either write a box office big hit or a box office flop. You are the lead actor or actress and you have a starring role. You are writing the script of your life each and every day. You have the power to create a new chapter. If you don't like the movie that's playing out in your life right now, I urge you to get focused and become committed to watching a new movie. You have the power to write a new script.

Commitment requires you to be extremely focused and disciplined in your daily routines and habits. I read a quote that says "discipline is the bridge between goals and accomplishments." With "reality television," social media, social life, toxic relationships, video games, all the new technology and the amount of information that we are required to process daily, people everywhere are falling victim to mass distraction. People are overwhelmed with distractions that serve to keep us discouraged and unfocused. There are a number of external and internal distractions that cause us to feel overwhelmed. Our job is to limit the amount of distractions that we allow to enter into our lives. Being distracted takes a toll on our decision-making process, affects our self-esteem, health, and productivity. I encourage you to discipline yourself and focus on what matters. Only focus on things or people that will contribute to your level of productivity.

You have to be committed to consciously put forth the effort to block out distractions. You can utilize self-discipline to defeat both internal and external interruptions. With external distractions, I practice the habit of turning off my smart phone and disconnecting from social media. I've found that it is very beneficial to turn my cell phone off at times as it allows me to improve my performance throughout the day. Same applies to the television, don't turn it on. You have to be fully committed to tuning out the negativity. With internal distractions, I put forth a lot of effort into controlling what urges I am acting on. I choose not to react to negative, troublesome people or situations.

Now let's recap, Television, don't turn it on. Social media, don't log on. Negativity, don't carry on. When you have a problem with any of the aforementioned situations yet you fail to place effort into changing them, you forfeit your right to complain because you are upholding the status quo. You too are a part of the distraction thus displaying your lack of commitment to change. You are in your own way. Get out of your own way and get focused on what truly matters. Get focused on things that truly add value to your life. Stop being distracted by things that hold no value.

Reduce the number of factors that contribute to stress in your life. I address social media a lot in this chapter because social media and this new technology is a gift and a curse. It's a gift when used correctly to market and operate businesses and share messages that promote positiveness and change and to keep in contact with family and friends. It's a curse when it's used incorrectly and becomes a stress factor that steals time, contentment, and joy away from you. I can admit that I have been guilty of scrolling through numerous social media networks for countless hours. I'll start by looking at a picture on Facebook and then I'll click on a tag of a person I might know. Then I'll find myself on that person's friend's, mother's, brother's, cousin's Auntie's page hours later. I know I'm not the only one that this has happened to. I had to tighten up and commit to having laser sharp focus. Technology can affect our health as well. Staring at screens for extended periods of time is not healthy for our eyes or bodies. With the increase of hand-held devices comes an increased risk of muscle fatigue, headaches, skin disorders and even cancer from the radio frequency exposure. Meanwhile, people experience a decrease in productivity, impersonal relationships, and their overall health and quality of life decrease.

I encourage you to make a commitment to exercise self-discipline in your daily habits and routines. I agree with Tony Robbins quote that says, "Stay committed to your decisions, but stay flexible in your approach." The difference between Successful People and unsuccessful people is the way that time is utilized.

Limit the number of distractions that you allow to interfere with your life. I've found that people that have achieved high levels of success discipline themselves not to allow distractions to interrupt them while working towards their goals and dreams. For instance, Warren Buffet, the second wealthiest person in the United States, doesn't use a cell phone.

Successful people are extremely focused and disciplined in how they use their time. Time is one of our most precious commodities. We all have 86,400 seconds per day. The way we spend our time determines the level of success that we have. At times we look at things that others are doing or things that others have and we compare ourselves and begin to feel inadequate. I encourage you not to waste one second focusing on someone else or things that do not matter. Commit to focusing on your unique gifts, purpose, being genuinely positive, and cultivating your dreams and goals. Focus on your capacity to love, be happy, serve, and contribute. Work hard to take care of yourself mentally, physically, spiritually, emotionally, and financially. In doing so, you will better position yourself to not only compete but to Win the race of life.

Chapter 13

Winning Principle #5
Set Goals/ Make Plans/ Organize

"All success comes from completed task"
John Asseraf

5. Set Goals/Make plans/Organize Socrates once said,

"An undisciplined life is an insane life."

Goals are described as the object of a person's effort, ambition or desired result. It is essential that you set goals for yourself. One of my favorite quotes about having goals is by my mentor, Les Brown. He said that "Goals are like a road map; they give you direction, yet many of us just drift along with no goals and no plan for life."

Your goals or lack thereof affect every area of your life. Goals affect your career, relationships, your attitude, your dress code, your mannerisms and almost every area of your life. A lot of high achievers set personal and career goals. It is important to do so that you do not become complacent in life. The saying goes, "People without goals get used by people who have them so make sure that you are clear about what you want out of life."

Make a to-do list by prioritizing high and low importance items. Make a list of your goals and don't be scared to dream big. I am a very ambitious person. I set high goals for myself. My dreams and goals are so big that they make me nervous at times. Your dreams and goals should make you nervous. Les Brown said it best, "A lot of people fail in life not because they aim too high and miss. They fail because they aim too low and hit." I encourage you to aim for the stars and the moon and even if you miss you'll land in a different space than you are currently in.

You have to be disciplined. Setting goals and accomplishing them requires a high level of self-discipline. Make a schedule. Set goals with time restraints. Focus on accomplishing one goal at a time. Put forth your maximum effort into achieving your goals. While attempting to reach your goals, no matter how challenging it seems to get, "Don't give in, Don't give up."

Your goals should be an everyday part of your life. Think about your dream, visualize your goals. Focus on fulfilling your goals. Visualize yourself achieving your goals. You need to have both short and long-term structured goals. You can set short-term goals that lead up to your long-term goal.

For instance, short-term goals are goals for tomorrow, this week, this month, this year. Long term goals are for 3-5 years. Make a list of the things you want to do, the places you want to go, the things you want to attain. I used a series of short-term goals that guided me to the attainment of my long-term goal. When you visualize your goal, you better position yourself to see them coming to pass.

You have to allow yourself time and be patient while you cultivate your dreams and goals. You must have patience and understand that nothing happens overnight. It takes time for dreams to be built. Things will not happen in your timing but in accordance with our higher power's timing.

When you allow yourself time to visualize, you open up your mind to a world of possibilities. When I was a kid, I used to visualize basic stuff such as lots of toys and game rooms in secret rooms in my house. No one taught me how to take the time to envision the life I wanted to live. I feel that it is vital that we take the time to do visualization exercises ourselves and with our children. The practice of visualization is extremely powerful. Visualization provides us with a blank canvas needed to design the life of our dreams. There is a value in seeing, believing, and achieving. We must be encouraged and encourage our children to possess dreams so big it makes their heart flutter when they think about them. No dream is too big. Visualize it, actualize it; it is possible to achieve the goals and dreams that are placed in your heart and mind. The sky is not the limit because there is still infinite space in space. There are truly no limitations in life.

I've been goal oriented all my life. I remember as a youngster I used to set goals to earn specific amounts of money. My sister Nikki and I would benefit from the weather no matter the season. When it was winter, we shoveled snow. During the spring, we picked worms for the fishers when it would rain. In the summer, we would collect and return bottles to the store for the deposit and run errands for our elders. And every fall we went door to door raking plenty of leaves. We always set out on our missions with a financial goal that we wanted to achieve. And we did, in fact, accomplish our goal 90% of the time. I didn't realize it at the time, but we were using goal setting skills at a very young age.

No matter what I was facing, I continued to set goals for myself all throughout my life because I wanted to attain specific achievements. You have the power to accomplish your goals regardless or not if there is one piece of evidence around to support it. As long as you are disciplined and work consistently towards your goal, it can be achieved.

Plan

I used my mind to think of ideas and different strategies that could help me change my situation. Things didn't just happen for me overnight; I planned this. I planned to overcome the challenges that I faced. I planned to beat my odds. I planned to live the lifestyle that I am living. I want you to make a plan to overcome all challenges in your mind and in your life to reach your goals.

Where would you like to be tomorrow, next week or next month? Where would you like to be 3 to 5 years from now? What is your plan of action to make it happen? Writing your goals down shows that you are serious about accomplishing your goals. Write down your goals then make three to four bullet points underneath each goal with a plan of action and how you will attain your major goals. I like to apply the S.M.A.R.T concept that I learned in Lakeview Shock

Incarceration Correctional Facility. Make sure each bullet point is specific, measurable, attainable, realistic, and timely. For instance, if your major goal is to become a public speaker some bullet points might be:

-Attend speakers training by April 21, 2017

*Research speaker training in your area

*Sign up for speaker training

*Attend speaker training

-Join local Toast Masters by June 30, 2017

*Locate nearest toastmasters club

*Attend a toastmasters meeting

*Meet toastmasters club members, learn about the organization

All of those small steps are Specific Measurable Attainable Realistic and Timely tasks that will help you to attain your major goal of becoming a public speaker. By managing goals the S.M.A.R.T way it increases the chances of your goals being reached. Being specific, setting metrics, focusing on attainment and setting realistic target dates for your goals is imperative to your success.

Organize

Don't pull you into many directions at once. Limit the number of goals you are working on at once and be aware of idle wants. Having organization allows your life to flow a lot smoother. Being organized reduces stress, mind clutter, and the anxiety of being overwhelmed. It also helps you to manage your time, helps you become more effective and efficient, helps you control your life so you can use your skills and talents better. And it sets a great example for your children so they can pick up the habit of being organized too. I encourage you to start getting organized today. There are a number of resources online, YouTube videos and free templates that can assist you in this area. You can even hire a professional organizer if you need to. You can use free resources such as Google Calendar, Google Drive, Dropbox, Picasa, Any.do, Daylio, Myfitnesspal and Mint to help you stay organized in all areas of your life.

Goals are ever-changing so always be open to making necessary adjustments to your goals. Make improvement a mandatory part of your life. Always work hard and never give up. Set goals for yourself and act now. Don't wait five years from now to realize that you are occupying the same space year after year, being who you don't want to be, living where you don't want to live, looking how you don't want to look, wearing what you don't want to wear, feeling how you don't want to feel.

I want you to make a commitment to yourself that you will start planning, organizing, and working just as hard on your own goals as you do your employer goals. I know you heard it before, "If you don't plan you are planning to fail." Set your mind on a Goal, develop an action plan, and crush it.

Chapter 14

Winning Principle #6
Practice

"Practice creates confidence; confidence empowers you"
~Simone Biles

6. Practice - You can become proficient in a skill or activity

when you exercise it persistently.

What differentiates doers from sayers is their daily habits and

routines. Doers go out and develop habits of success. Sayers

talk about going out developing habits of success.

A major key to success is to practice relentlessly. Practice makes it permanent. Sharpen your sword read, write, attend conferences, workshops, live streams, webinars, conference calls, etc. Network and connect with people who have the knowledge that you need. With today's technology there are numerous tools and resources available to you at no cost.

The more you practice, the more you become conditioned to living your desired way of life. The more you practice, the less you'll dread doing it. It is said that "It is better to be prepared and not have an opportunity than to have an opportunity and not be prepared." Do not wait until an opportunity presents itself to start practicing. You have to love yourself enough to work on your dreams and goals whether you have an opportunity or not.

Use your time wisely. Jim Rohn Says, "You don't get paid by the hour. You get paid for the value you bring to the hour." Time is one of life's most valuable assets. We have to use it to serve us, instead of us chasing behind time running late constantly attempting to catch up to life. That was me for a number of years I practiced very poor time management skills. I have gotten better with time. I have to admit I was always that person that would arrive late every single time no variations.

The turning point for me with being disrespectful of time was when my 10-year-old niece confronted me about being late. My sister called me from work and asked me to take my niece to the hairdresser because her initial ride backed out. I agreed. Her appointment was at 2:30 I got her to her appointment at 2:45pm. On the way there she said, "Auntie, my Auntie Kat said, 'you have to be on time places because when you don't, it shows that you don't respect the other person time." Boom, I felt smaller than a fairy-fly. I said, "yes, that is true" while rushing to change the subject. Here it is my ten-year-old niece who knows the value of time and the importance of respecting other people's time, yet I'm a 35-year-old woman late everywhere I go. I had to do better from that day forward. I have been more conscious of my time management. In doing so, I found that I was able to get more accomplished by practicing better time management. Also, I found that being on time helped me become more organized and reduced my level of frustration and stress related to running late.

The act of improving your time management begins with making a decision to manage your time effectively. You have to decide that you will be committed to being on time. Leadership guru Brian Tracy teaches that by reciting positive affirmations, having faith and belief in the affirmations will result in your subconscious mind accepting and living out your affirmations. For example, if you continuously late repeat: "I am an excellent manager of time. I am an excellent manager of time. I am an excellent manager of time." What you are decreeing will be established in your external behaviors.

The practice of prioritization of time is a major element in creating a winning lifestyle. We must spend our time on the things that will yield us the highest return on our investment. It is said that practicing 10,000 hours of something makes you an expert in that field. Winning is a product of consistent practice.

Stagnation is a silent dream killer. When I stopped lying to myself and truly started practicing and working, then and only then is when I began to win my desired results in life.

People are accustomed to doing the same thing over and over and over again. Don't be one of those people, break the cycle of complacency and make practicing your dreams and goals a regimen. The fact of the matter is that if you don't want it bad enough, you will not do what it takes to get it. However, when you possess an unyielding desire to achieve your goals and dreams, then you will practice vigorously until you win you heart's desires.

When you are disciplined, you will reap the reward. Always go the extra mile and practice even when no one tells you to. You are giving yourself an advantage when you make a habit of taking the personal initiative to practice. The key is to find a balance with practicing and regularly scheduled daily activities. It's imperative to sharpen your sword constantly; however, be careful not to exhaust yourself to the point where what you're practicing begins to turn you off.

When you truly understand your purpose, you will place practice as a high priority in your life. We have to make sure we are being strategic in what we are practicing. We can put a lot of time and effort into practice, but if we are not practicing on our assignment from our higher power, our efforts will not bear any fruit. For me, I choose to set certain days to practice certain things. For instance, Monday, Wednesday, and Friday were my days to practice my speeches and coaching. Tuesday & Thursday were my days to practice for my videos. Saturday was my day to record my videos. Sunday was my day to plan and practice for the upcoming week.

My goal was to be a published Author, Motivational/ Inspirational Speaker and a Life Coach. I knew I could not rub the side of an oil lamp and a genie would grant me those three desires. I had to focus on my goals and practice and work hard every single day to achieve my goals. I practiced all that I could. Every single day I made deposits into myself. I listened to motivational speakers such as Les Brown, Zig Ziggler, Eric Thomas, John Assaraf, Tony

Robbins, Lisa Nichols, Jim Rohn, Inky Johnson, Stevan Covey and more. I watched their videos repeatedly on YouTube, DVD, attended webinars, listened to podcast, conference calls, and attended live training. I studied sermons from Pastor Td Jakes, Joel Osteen, Pastor Stevan Furtick, etc. I researched statics, quotes, and stories pertaining to the topic that I desired to speak about. I practiced relentlessly and continue to do so to date. When I spend time on social media networks, I make sure I'm being productive by reading positive information or learning how to use the platforms to add value to my goals and dreams. I practiced my skills and activities until they became a permanent part of my life. I am no different than you are, so you can do the same. Don't ponder on doing it. Just take action. Your ability to practice will differentiate whether your contribution will be ordinary or extraordinary.

Chapter 15

Winning Principle #7
Execute

"When you're not spending any time worrying, you're spending time executing"
~Gary Vaynerchuk

7. Execute- You can have ideas be smart, talented and skilled. However, your success lies in your ability to execute.

The key to getting anything done is simply just to do it. Don't think about it for too long because you will think yourself out of it. Just act on it. Procrastination is our arch enemy. I encourage you to fight the urge to procrastinate. Get up and do it even when you do not feel like it because the results of getting the task done will be worth it in the end.

A lot of people sleepwalk their way through life. I've been guilty of daydreaming about completing a task that I should have completed minutes, hours, days or even months ago. Why is that? Lack of value for the task? Lack of motivation? Laziness, fear, and complacency are common reasons why people procrastinate. You can overcome procrastination by first acknowledging that you are doing it. Secondly, assessing the level of importance of the task. Thirdly addressing why you are behaving this way. Lastly, develop strategies that will allow you to overcome procrastination. One of the most effective strategies is just to take action.

Motivational Speaker Eric Thomas said, "Execution in business is like a heart beating as it relates to your body, once the heart stops that's it for your body." When you fail to execute, you are unconsciously setting yourself up for disappointment. The same applies to your personal life. You should always carry out plans of action and have progressive movement, development, and advancement in your life. A lot of people cheat themselves out of being successful because of their failure to execute. We all have the same ideas, the only difference between you and the person that executed their idea is that they acted on the idea and you have not yet. It is not too late to put your goals and dreams into action. Protect your energy. Rid your life of complainers also known as energy drainers. The only person that is stopping you is you. Stop wasting your time blaming and complaining because those types of actions are draining. Place all your energy and effort into changing and executing. You have the power to carry out a new plan of action. Don't stay stagnate. Keep going no matter what.

Execution allows you to stay encouraged in the midst of discouraging circumstances. By being an action taker, you will learn how to use problems to propel you into positions of power. Being an aggressive action taker is one of the main ingredients I used in my recipe for overcoming any of life's challenges. I kept going no matter what I was faced with. When things were going wrong in my life, I kept pushing forward. I didn't stop and get stuck in the darkness; I kept moving towards the light. I kept taking action no matter how bad things seemed, no matter how much pain I was in, no matter how tough the situation was. I made a plan and acted on it. I discovered that my power lies in my ability to act; my power lies in my ability to withstand the pain in order to keep pushing forward to change my circumstances. You must have an action plan in place and act on it.

Intended behavior is not enough to get the job done. You must possess enacted behavior to produce execution. Make an ideal, dream a dream, plan for it, execute it, make it a reality. Get creative. Stop focusing on what you don't have and use what you do have to get the job done. Don't worry about who you don't have in your corner or what you don't have, just execute and God will align you with the right people at the right time—just take action! Your ability to execute will liberate you and take you to the next level in life.

Inspiration and motivation are dead without execution. It is human nature to want to see immediate results once you execute. After you execute, you must develop a strong sense of patience combined with persistence, commitment, and faith. The story of the Chinese Bamboo tree displays the importance of having the aforementioned qualities. Chinese farmers planted seeds and care for them. Each and every day the Chinese farmer watered the spots where he placed them. They place their faith in all the Bamboo tree will provide once it grows. They water and fertilize the seeds year after year, and nothing happens. It is watered and fertilized every single day for four years straight with no progress. Then in the fifth year, the Bamboo tree sprouts up. It sprouts up over 90ft high. The Bamboo tree didn't just grow that high over a six-week period, it took five years. I tell you this story to show you how everything will not happen as quickly as you want it to happen and when it doesn't, don't feel discouraged, don't lose hope, don't quit. Just keep watering and fertilizing your goals and dreams and stay in faith. All of your small actions have an impact. You might not see the change or growth immediately, but it will happen. Stay in faith, have patience and perseverance, and you will see your end result come to pass.

You have to stop over-thinking everything. Stop trying to be perfect to execute. Stop playing it safe because your hesitation to progress in life is causing you more pain. You have to recondition your mindset and train yourself to break through obstacles and be unstoppable. Once you challenge your self-limiting beliefs and become aware of your innate ability to conquer your fears, you will continue to draw on your power. It's solely up to you. Don't allow fear to prevent you from taking action. Push yourself no matter what. Accept and embrace temporary setbacks and defeats as it is part of the process.

Make it a habit to start a task, focus on the task intensely, check the daily progress, and finish the task that you started. Every now and then stop and check your progress. I'm not saying waste time by being distracted by constantly googling your own name to use that as a measurement of progress. That is not an accurate measurement of progress. A good way to determine if progress is being made is to make a checklist daily and observe if the actions that you are indulging in every day are getting you any closer to fulfilling your goals.

When developing your personal, professional or business goals, execution is one of the most important elements of your project. You have the ability and power to carry out your goals and dreams. It is possible for you to complete your vision. I encourage you to start and finish.

Epilogue

I wrote this book in efforts to help others cultivate a winning mindset and lifestyle for themselves. I wanted to provide people with information, strategies and techniques that would enable them to overcome life challenges. I began by giving you a synopsis of my upbringing and my background so that you can see that I didn't begin with a silver spoon in my mouth. I had to make important decisions and work hard to change my thought process and for every accomplishment in life. You too can overcome life's challenges by deciding to change your life. By getting focused, changing your mindset, changing your attitude, changing your environment and upgrading your relationships. By being ambitious and putting forth your greatest effort to create positive change in your life.

The When|Win Approach encourages you to just do it. To act on and execute your goals and dreams. Don't wait until you can see everything lining up for yourself with your own eyesight. Act on your mind sight. When you can dream it, you can make it your reality. Walk out on faith and you will carry out dreams that you thought were impossible. You heard my story. It doesn't matter who you are, what you been through or what you are going through, God will use you like God used me. God doesn't only call the qualified he qualifies the called.

Always have confidence in who you are and what you do. Don't wait until everything is perfect to be happy, seek happiness daily. Don't settle where you are. Don't settle for being mediocre, you are full of potential. Stop playing small, stop discrediting yourself. Don't sit back consumed by fear because you are qualified. You have the power in you to

160

overcome any situation and live the life of your dreams. I believe in you! I want you to discard your current belief system and write a new chapter for yourself. I want you to decide today to be your best personally, spiritually, professionally and in every area of your life.

Know that nothing worked out for me for a long time. I suffered from bouts of depression, I met rejection from job after job, however, I did not quit. When you don't quit, you will see your desired result come to pass. Keep moving forward no matter what, don't let anyone or anything stop you. When something doesn't go the way you planned don't get discouraged, make another plan. When I was released from prison I faced a lot of rejection, it was tough. I had to decide not to get discouraged and to use that rejection as fuel to keep driving me forward. I have encountered struggle, loss, defeat and failure. Nothing worked for me until I understood that I am not the results that I produce. Failure is a part of the process, embrace it. Don't be scared to take risk in pursuit of your goals and dreams. The dream is most definitely real. It's nothing that we cannot do, have or be.

Never give up!! Stay focused, stay persistent, stay committed and stay in faith. I am not telling you that you will live a life that has no problems. Life is not easy. Life is challenging, however, you are strong enough to get through the challenges. It is worth it to face life's challenges and move forward. Life happens, you're going to experience major disappointments, heartache, and pain, however, just know that adversities will come and go. The pain will come and go. Don't let anything or anyone destroy you. I urge you to acknowledge your problems, embrace them and move forward. Stop allowing life's challenges to immobilize you. The When|Win Approach gives you The formula to overcome life's challenges. You can live the life of your dreams. You will Win "not if" But When you believe that it is possible for you to do so.

I Believe In You,

LaShaundria Coleman

ABOUT THE AUTHOR

Born and raised in Niagara Falls, New York, LaShaundria Coleman graduated from Buffalo State College with a Bachelor's of Science degree in Sociology.

LaShaundria Coleman is the daughter of Zettie "Smith" Perry and William Coleman. She is the stepdaughter of the late Charles Perry. She has eight sisters and four brothers. LaShaundria lives in Charlotte, North Carolina with her son Jimmie. She enjoys traveling, writing, reading, cooking and empowering others.

LaShaundria Coleman is a life-long learner and serial entrepreneur that has owned and operated a number of businesses. She looks forward to traveling the world and empowering people with her inspirational authentic messages of positive change, perseverance and bouncing back from tough situations. Her delivery is deeply passionate and convicting, it leaves her audiences captivated.

If you want to know when LaShaundria's next book will come out, please visit her website at http://www.lashaundriacoleman.com, where you can sign up to receive free promotional items and an email when she has her next release.